11 WAYS TO A BEAUTIFUL LIFE

A GUIDE TO EXPERIENCE BEAUTY OF LIFE

PRITMA JASHNANI

ISBN 979-888591560-1

I Dedicate this book to all those people who take life for granted and do not feel grateful for all things in life which they have.

Contents

Preface

Have we ever realized that we always keep complaining without being grateful for all that we are already bestowed with?

We compare our lives with others, and do not make attempt to improve our own life. We are in a habit of imitating others to gain success by the same method forgetting that life is a difficult exam in which everyone has a different question paper, so obviously the answers would be different.

We earn money to satisfy our needs and sometimes we are so blinded by the urge of earning more money that we forget to enjoy every moment of our life.

When something does not go according to our will in life, we become frustrated and depressed. Here we make a mistake, as we forget that whatever happens in life is with the will of God. He knows better than us what to give and when to give.

When we are in a relationship, it is necessary to talk and get to know each other. Transparency is necessary in a relationship for it to last long. The care and attention that we give to a relationship makes it strong and deep.

The failures in life should be taken positively as they are the first step to success. A Failure teaches us not to commit any mistakes further.

Sometimes in our lives, we meet people who do not care for us, then it's better to leave them and move ahead in life. Instead of taking revenge, it is better to forgive them and not to create toxicity in ourselves.

To live a beautiful life, its better also to spend some time with ourselves and get to know more about ourselves.

Expectations are the root causes of all our miseries. So stop expecting from people and be your own support and live a happy life.

Acknowledgements

I express my sincere gratitude to my late mother, late brother, my father and my sisters, without whom it was not possible to express my thoughts in the form of words written in this book.

Though my mother is not with us, but her blessings and love always remains with us.She had a belief that one day I will be writing books and become an author.

I also express my gratitude to my mentor **Inspiring Jatin** under whose guidance, I could actually make my wish of becoming an author come true.

CHAPTER ONE

GRATITUDE

Imagine we land on some planet that has no air, water, and natural vegetation. Will we be able to survive No, not even for a second. How do you feel after imagining? It is suffocating! Right.

We as humans are so lucky to have been born on Earth. The Earth has an abundance of natural resources for us. We have fresh air to breathe in, water resources to quench our thirst, land to live in, and natural vegetation to satisfy our hunger. These resources are available to us right from our birth and are always available to us. Do we ever feel grateful for all these resources in our life? Truly, things that come easily are not valued. So is with us. We do not pay gratitude to all these abundant resources that Earth has given us and that too without paying a single penny. This is the greatest gift bestowed on us by the Universe.

We are never conscious of the way we are exploiting these resources for our purpose.

- We are cutting trees for our needs, which is reducing the amount of oxygen supply around us.
- We waste a lot of water daily while brushing or taking a bath, as we keep taps open and water is being wasted uselessly.
- We waste a lot of food and throw it away, without realizing that many people are longing for this food.

- We are polluting the air with the fumes of factories and automobiles.
- We are throwing waste materials in the rivers and oceans, without realizing that these waters are brought to our houses through taps.

Let me share here a small story.

There was an old man who was on a ventilator and was undergoing treatment in a hospital. When he got well, he received a bill for the ventilator from the doctor. As soon as he received the bill, he started crying. The doctor took pity on him and said, "I would reduce the bill. Please don't be so emotional". But you know what that old man answered?

The old man said, "I am not crying for the bill that I have to pay for my treatment. I am crying that for so many years nature had been so much merciful to us. It had given an unlimited supply of oxygen to us. Nature gave water to us. It gave air to us and that too free of cost for which we did not have to pay any bills or any money. Despite that, we people have never been thankful to nature".

What does this story tell us? We have so much in abundance provided by the universe that we are still to realize the importance of all these things. We should always be grateful for the things and the resources we have at our disposal.

Everyone wants to be happy in life. We want a perfect family, a good job, high social status. In pursuing things that would make us happy, we forget that we are living a life of illusion. Do we ever stop and think that Universe has given us so much that we do not realize it and never pay gratitude for it?

Research says anyone can be happy in this world if they inculcate the practice of gratitude. Being thankful for every little thing can help us in every area of our life.

When we are thankful to the universe for every moment of life, we experience that; in return, the universe gives us more. This is the magic of gratitude. When you are passing through difficult phases of your life, it does not mean that everything is over, rather shift your focus to other beautiful things around you, nature, the birds, the trees, the family, the friends, who love and care for you, a house to live in, the food to eat, the air we breathe in.

Isn't it beautiful that we wake up the next day alive? Truly, we get a new life every day. Let us thank God for every new day we wake up.

Let us see the effects of Gratitude :-

1) Take a pause and see the environment around, the sun, the sky, the atmosphere, nature itself and thank each of these things for serving us and you will feel a surge of energy.

2) When we express gratitude, we become more optimistic, as the brain releases dopamine (a neurotransmitter, to pleasure and happiness) and serotonin(to help regulate mood).

3) When we take a bath, always express gratitude to the water which is being provided for bathing. Water listens, to everything and will respond that way. You will feel fresher after bathing.

4) Gratitude helps to improve mental health. People who feel thankful for each and everything in their life, experience a reduction in the stress hormone (cortisol). It also reduces the chances of cardiac arrest and even eases negative experiences.

So it is necessary to experience gratitude towards all the little things in life. This will also improve our mental health and give us happiness.

5) Express gratitude to God before going to bed for all the good things and events you had come across that day, and whatever you have achieved, and you will get a sound sleep.

6) Whenever you express gratitude towards anybody, you feel that the stress level reduces, and anxiety and depression are nowhere in life.

7) Before having food, pay gratitude to God and to your mother or the cook who has made it with noble efforts. Even thank all the factors responsible for making food available at your table. Never disrespect the food. If you do not feel like eating, do not throw it away. Either feed an animal or someone poor.

8 Express gratitude to the situations or the people who have been responsible for you to attain some position in life. While expressing gratitude, it is necessary to be free from ego.

9) Be thankful for the human body you have. Every morning, when you get up, rub both your palms to create warmth and massage every part of your body, expressing gratitude that your body is whole and working. As many people around us may miss some part of their bodies. Some may have lost their arms, while others may have lost their eyes, some are suffering from the disease. So if you are healthy, be thankful for your body.

"This beautiful morning, let us thank God for having woken up us Hale and healthy and be grateful for every breath that we take. Many people might not have seen this morning, so take every moment of your life as a blessing of God."

Pritma

10) Always be grateful to your parents, who have taken great pains and made so many sacrifices to see you attaining a prominent position in life. Never forget them when you attain a prominent position. They are the ones who cared for you in your times of need. Be always available to them.

A small exercise for you

- Make a list of all the things you have for which you had never asked for. Write it in your diary and thank the universe for everything you have.
- Always before having food, thank making it available to you. the universe for
- Always thank the water before bathing by saying, "I love you and thank you for being there to cleanse my body ". See what you experience.

Summary

- Be grateful for abundant natural resources provided by nature.
- Be grateful for your body, which is healthy.
- Be grateful to God for providing you with food and shelter.
- Be grateful to your parents who helped you attain a high position.
- Be grateful to all people who help you.
- Paying gratitude reduces stress levels and reduces the chances of a heart attack.

CHAPTER TWO

BELIEVE IN YOURSELF

What is belief?

Faith in something or someone is belief.

Like a child believes in his parents and follows whatever they teach it. Some people have beliefs in their religious rituals etc. Have you ever thought, when a father throws his child in the air, the child laughs? Why? The reason is that it has faith in its father that he will not let it fall?

A. What about believing in yourself?

Yes, this is a topic about believing in yourself. If you do not have faith or trust in your decisions or actions, then you will always depend on others to decide or make choices for you. It would be like cattle, having no power of taking decisions, led by their master, wherever he leads them to.

Let me share a story with you. ________________________________

Have you heard of Arunima Sinha? She is a sportswoman who is a seven-time Indian volleyball player and is the first woman to climb Mount Everest with a prosthetic leg. She is the daughter of an army man. Born in Ambedkar Nagar, Uttar Pradesh.In April 2011, she had boarded Padmavati express to give her CSIF examination. However, something unfortunate happened to her. The robbers who tried to snatch her bag and gold chain pushed her off the train. As soon as she fell on the railway tracks, another train, coming at full speed, had crushed her leg below the knee. She was suffering there for several hours, then carried to the hospital. The Doctors had to amputate her leg to save her life. They declared that she could never play volleyball. During her treatment, Indian cricketer Yuvraj, who fought the battle against cancer, inspired her.

With her strong will power, she climbed Mount Everest, and that too with her prosthetic leg. Not only did she climb Mount Everest, but also many other mountains like Mount Kilimanjaro, Mount Elbrus and so on.

In 2015, the Indian Government honored her with the Padma Shri award.

Isn't it an amazing story of a woman who believed in herself and made a name for herself? This is because she tapped her innate hidden powers. She is the creator of her destiny. She could have sat back home with an amputated leg and led an ordinary life, but she chose to be the Arjuna of her life's battle.

"Remember, you are the Krishna and Arjuna in your battle of life. Emerge victorious by remaining consistent in your belief **" . Pritma**

The Almighty has given man innate powers, which man has to explore for himself and be the creator of his destiny.

Have you ever seen why a lion is the king of the jungle, though there are more powerful, clever, and agile animals than the lion? An elephant is the most powerful animal. Wolf is the cleverest animal. Giraffe is the tallest animal, yet none of them but the lion being lazy, not so powerful, not the cleverest, not the tallest of all, is the king of the jungle?

This is because the lion believes in himself that he is the king and no one can beat him in the jungle. This belief creates the attitude of being the king, and because of his attitude, when he takes action and attacks the animals, he appears ferocious that even the most powerful animal, the elephant, fears him.

Similarly, if you start believing yourself, your attitude will change, and your brain will help you take action to achieve your goals. Try it and see the results.

Throw away all the fears and nervousness within you. You are born to achieve goals in life, to live a happy and beautiful life. For this, remove your hesitations, come out of your comfort zone, start taking action and you will lead a happy and satisfying life.

So what, if you fail in your first attempt to achieve your goal? At least you will learn from your mistakes and then with double energy, you can go for it.

Try the following and see the difference

- **Believe in your appearance-**

Stop depending on others to compliment you or pass remarks on your looks. It does not make any difference, even if you are dark in complexion or are short. You might fumble when speaking or are not attractive; you might not be much educated. The thing that matters is if you believe in yourself that you can attain great heights, you will be the creator of your beautiful life.

There is a list of people who used to stutter, yet have achieved prominent positions in life, like

1. **Joseph Biden**–Former US Senator and Vice President of the USA.
2. **Winston Churchill**–British Prime Minister.
3. **Mel Tillis**–Country Singer.

And this list goes on and on.

Many people were not so good-looking but have been famous, and people still remember them, like -

1. **Michael Jackson**–the famous dancer and singer.
2. **Steven Tyler**–the greatest living Rock songwriters.

And this list goes on and on.

They all believed in themselves and have attained great heights.

- **Do not step back.**

Some people may try to discourage you. They may try to hurt you and you may quit or give up. Instead, take no notice of them. Keep moving towards achieving your goals. Behave as if you are alone in your path. Do not retreat, but give your 200% and show the world that your belief has made you win.

If you face Rejections, it does not mean you are not a worthy person. There are millions of people out there who might respect and value your talent.

Let us see an example-

Albert Einstein – Who discovered the Theory of Relativity had to undergo various discouragements in life. Till the age of four, he could not speak properly. When he went to school, the teachers called him lazy as they did not understand his questions. He did not step back and went on doing research.

If you believe in yourself, no one can stop you.

- **Make affirmations before going to bed**

Make affirmations, visualize that you have already achieved your goals. This will program your subconscious mind and it will guide you to the path to achieve your goals.

- **Be authentic**

Do not imitate others to achieve success. Be the person you are. Do not get distracted by others and take the wrong path to achieve your goals. No matter how much time it takes. Gradually you will gain success. You cannot copy exactly the success path of others. Maybe the path taken by others might not be the right path for you. You can take inspiration, but ultimately believing in yourself will make your path to success.

- **Keep the company of friends who are well-wishers.**

Do not discuss everything with your friends until you have achieved your goal.

- **Keep a positive attitude.**

If something goes wrong, do not be upset. Always think positive that things will get better and you are going to achieve your goal one day. Remember, all things, all problems, are temporary. They will go as they have come. They will disappear one day, just like every moment of our life is not the same. So do not take things seriously. Nothing is permanent, not even your worries.

- **Do not lose confidence, even in adverse situations.**

Even when situations are not favorable, do not get disheartened. Do not lose faith in yourself.

Let us see an example.

Benjamin Franklin– Franklin was a school dropout. His parents could not afford education expenses, but did not give up, and read books like crazy. He discovered bifocals and lightning rods. He had to leave studies after class 10, yet he did not get disheartened and made his niche.

What do we learn? No matter how adverse the conditions are, if you believe you can attain greater heights, the universe will open the doors for you. Ultimately you will lead a beautiful life.

Some exercises for you

- No matter how look or how you speak, do not be ashamed. Instead, be confident of yourself and be proud that you a precious gift of the Universe. This will change your attitude and perspective towards life.

- If anybody speaks against you, give deaf ears to them and tell them that you already know, as this makes you special from others.

- If you have any dream to fulfill, always make an affirmation before sleep, visualizing that you have already achieved it. This will boost your confidence level.

Summary

- Do not get discouraged if people comment on your appearance.

- Believe in yourself while making decisions and you will attain success.

- Do not get disheartened when you face rejections. Believe in yourself that they will accept it one day.

- Make affirmations before going to bed that you have already achieved your goals and you will feel the difference.

- Do not imitate others. You may take inspiration, but make your path.

CHAPTER THREE

MAINTAINING RELATIONSHIPS

What is a relation?

A bond that we share with anyone, be it a family member, a friend, a spouse, etc. If we have good relationship, our life becomes stress free and we can lead a satisfied life. If there are tensions in any relations, we become stressed and this distracts our mind from our goals.

Right from our birth we own blood relations with our father, mother, brothers and sisters. Apart from this, we make relations with some other people like making friends, having a love relationship with a boy and girl, having good relations with our neighbors. If we are in business, then we try having good relations with our clients and customers.

We are sociable beings who cannot exist in isolation. How we keep great relationships with our friends, family members, and others is in our control .For this, we need to understand that every human born on the earth is unique. No one can be like the other .Being different from others, we have a different temperament. Some are happy-go persons, some are serious, and some always become furious at little things. One cannot change the nature of other person according to their own likes and dislikes. Nobody can change for others overnight. So it is our duty to see how to manage our relations with them ,which can be long lasting.

For husband and wife, there are clash of opinions as they may have different nature ,likes and dislikes .So it is necessary that they spend more time with each other to know each other, likes, dislikes, nature and be prepared to accept each other .After all it's a lifelong relationship that has to be carried on.

You can't just abandon each other because your personalities or likes and dislikes differ. Nobody can compare to you, as I have stated. As time passes, you become accustomed to each other's personalities. Relationships should always be guided by the soul rather than by routine.

Nobody is perfect in this world. If you accept your partner with all his/ her imperfections and care for them, then you are going to be an ideal couple. Every relationship requires care and attention.

"***Relations are like plants. The more care and attention you give to them, the deeper they become. The moment you stop giving attention, they wither away and become weak. Choice is yours how to grow your relationship***"

Pritma

- **Try to know Each other's likes and dislikes.**

It is vital to communicate with one another and learn about each other's likes and dislikes. You will become more open-minded and understanding of one another as a result of this

- **Hang Out With Each Other**

Whenever you are free, find time to go out together instead of hanging out with friends. This will bring you closer to each other and you care for each other.

- **Let Go Off The Ego**

The biggest problem in any relationship is ego. The more you promote your ego, the more distance you will create in your relationship. If one partner is ill, the other partner can take over his or her work. It is a part of life. We are a family. If you have this feeling, then you will never have the ego barring you from taking over his or her responsibility.

Suppose if you quarreled with each other, then you have to keep aside your ego and apologize to strengthen your relationship.

- **Try To Know Each Other's Weaknesses And Strengths**

Help your partner to come out of his or her weakness and turn it into strength instead of taunting your partner for his or her weakness. Be there to be their strengths.

- **Don't Hold Grudges Against Each Other.**

Remember, family members are not our enemies. So if you have any problem with each other, solve it by talking to each other and removing all the false notions against each other.

- **Give Your Children Time**

Whenever your children want to chat to you or tell you about their troubles or accomplishments. Always be available to them. Allow adequate time for them and pay attention to their accomplishments and issues. If any.

- **TryTo Understand the Interest Of Your Child**

If he or she has any other interests, such as dance, writing, music, or painting. Encourage them and let them learn new things rather than forcing your objectives or ambitions on them simply because you were unable to reach yours. Your objectives cannot be imposed on your children.

Try to figure out what they want to do with their lives because if you force your desires on them, they may turn out to be failures in life because they are uninterested in your goals. So talk to them and, once you know what they are interested in, encourage them to pursue it.

We have an exceptional example of India's top dancer, a girl named Saumya, who recently won from Sony Entertainment Television. Her father wished for her to become a physician. However, she developed a strong interest in belly dancing. Her mother supported her, but it took several months for her father to do so. He didn't even speak to her politely. When he watched her performing well at the performance and receiving praise from the judges on a regular basis. His mind was immediately altered, and he now has converted half of his clinic to his daughter's dance studio.

Isn't it a proud moment for a father to see his daughter take home the prize for India's best dancer? She was named the best dancer in India.

So if your child is interested in any art, you as parents should encourage them, you can give your children wings to soar above and take the entire sky for themselves.

- **Always Express Your Love To Your Children.**

Give individual attention to each of your child so that they feel loved. Surprise them by taking them out. Try to know the likes and dislikes. Always be there when they come from the school. Try to know how the day was, what they felt when they attended the school. Or was there something that had happened at school which had made them upset?

- **Encourage Your Child**

Pat your child's back for every improvement that he/she makes in life. Do not compare your child with anyone else's child. After all, all children cannot be toppers, but they can be prominent leaders, great motivational speakers, big business tycoons.

A certificate does not define how able you are. Many people who have attained MBA degrees ,are still searching for jobs, are still unemployed. Many people are college dropouts and are still doing well in their careers.

Bill Gates and **Steve Jobs** never finished their college and who doesn't know them .**Mark Zuckerberg** got his honorary degree from Harvard and that took 12 years after dropping from college just to build **Face book.**

This is proof that getting a certificate does not certify that your child is intelligent and able and can attain heights.

- **Look after yourself.**

Don't forget to look after yourself in the midst of looking after everyone else. Set aside time for yourself. Make an effort to exercise. Remember, if you're in good shape and mentally healthy, everything will fall into place.

- **Make Friends With Your Kids**

Some laws and regulations are required to place on your children in order to manage their conduct, but if your child makes a mistake, instead of reprimanding them, be friendly and attempt to understand the reasons and circumstances behind their mistakes. If you are friendly with your child, you will find that he will divulge his hidden secrets. Put yourself in your child's shoes to better comprehend how he or she feels. Consider your child's point of view. This will result in a strong tie between the parents and the children.

This is a proven and true fact from my childhood, when our mother and father were friendly with us. We didn't feel the need to hide anything because we were always willing to accept comments for the decisions we had made in our lives. To my parents, I am still proud to declare that I am an open book. Despite the fact that I have lost my mother, I am an open book to my father.

- **Sometimes You Have To Be Patient And Silent.**

When the other person is in an aggressive mood, it is better to be silent. When you are silent, you're giving a chance to the other person to make him regret it. It does not take arguments to prove that you are correct. When the other person calms down, you can talk to him and explain your points.

Remember one thing; to be silent always sometimes can be harmful, so you have to take a stand for yourself at times.

- **Don't try to overpower each other.**

Allow each other space. Do not overpower, since we are all human beings with the right to live freely. Nobody has the right to take away another's freedom. Respect and honor your partner's will.

- **Don't be envious of your partner's achievements.**

Respect him or her in all aspects of life, be a part of his or her celebrations, and encourage him or her to do their best, whether male or female.

Many women are forced to abandon their employment because their spouses are envious of their professional or entrepreneurial success.

What does it mean to be a life partner if you are one? A life partner is similar to a friend who collaborates with you. There's no need to try to outsmart one other or stifle each other's advancement.

It should be a source of pride for you if your partner is succeeding in his or her business. You should be proud of and happy for your partner's accomplishments. Who are we to affect each other by our actions when the universe treats all human beings equally, whether it is the Sun, the Moon, the Stars, the Air, the Water, or the Land? We have no right to take away another's freedom. Instead, I would advise you to give your wife wings to fly and assist her in making a name for her.

- **Respect and give time to your Elders**

Always find time to spend with your elders and try to know their needs and wishes. Take them for an outing. Do not make them feel alone. If they are suffering from any ailment, help them out with a Doctor and keep them active by helping them do exercises.

Remember the time when you could not take care of yourself, and your parents selflessly helped you to speak and grow up. Now is the time to repay them back.

"Your parents are your valuable assets that have helped you grow and whose experience and blessings will never fail you in your life"

Pritma

Some Exercise for you

- Always bid your children with a happy smile and welcome them when they come from school. Listen to their stories they want to share with you.

- Take care of your Elders and listen to them when they want to share experiences with you. Whatever they say, don't argue, first think then take action on their suggestions if you feel is okay.

- If anybody does not understand you, just be silent and keep yourself calm. Later explain that person your point of view.
- If your children are improving in their studies give them rewards to encourage them to do better. Do not impose your dreams on them. Let them choose their career according to their Interests.

Summary

1. All people are unique and cannot be like you.
2. Understand the temperament and perspective of other people and try managing your relations.
3. Give time to each of your child and make them feel loved.

4. Understand the weakness and strengths of your partner and help them come out of their weakness.
5. Respect your Partner's progress whether male or female and celebrate their success.
6. Do not overpower your partner to mould according to you.

CHAPTER FOUR

YOUR HABITS MAKE YOUR LIFE

What is a habit, exactly?

An action that we perform over and over until we are entirely acclimated to it is referred to as a habit. Giving up a habit is difficult.

Some people have a habit of intruding into the lives of others. Some people have a horrible tendency of deceiving others. Some people have a habit of boasting about their achievements.

It is easy to form bad habits, but it is much more difficult to break them. On the other hand, it is difficult to form good habits, but it is much easier to break them.

The type of environment and company you live in, has an impact on all of your habits. Young individuals, particularly if they are in bad company, are greatly affected.

Bad habits can be harmful to your health and can make you depressed. On the other side, good habits can assist you in leading a healthy lifestyle.

In this lesson, we'll talk about positive behaviors or what we say Good Habits..

- **Always Be Mindful of Yourself**

Instead of worrying about others, focus on yourself and your family. There are a number of difficulties in your environment and in your family that need to be addressed and resolved. In order to grow as a person, keep track of your goals, accomplishments, and flaws. Rather than worrying about others, trust me, you may live a happy and fulfilled life if you keep a check on yourself.

- **Make it a habit to use your phone as little as possible.**

Spend your time with those around you rather than looking at your phone. In your spare time, learn something new and make an attempt to improve your health. Take a vacation, visit the sights, swim, cycle, and do other activities, instead of flooding your mind with information from social media. This will allow you to be more creative and open-minded.

- **Get as much sleep as possible and rise as early as possible.**

Sleeping late has a negative impact on your physical and mental wellbeing. To get a decent night's sleep, do a 10-minute meditation or read a page or two of a book before bed. There will be no need for medicines because you will be stress-free and relaxed.

- **Stop Over thinking**

Over thinking might cause you to get more stressed and have a detrimental effect on your health. Take a pause and focus on other pleasurable aspects of your life if you are having trouble with anything and cannot seem to solve it, shift your attention from it to other good things like

A. Your family members who, no matter what, are always there for you.
C. Your body, which bears your weight all of the time and is nevertheless willing to help you do your goal.
C. Nature, such as trees, the sun, the moon, rivers, and so on,

This will inevitably lead to a solution to your problems by calming your mind and allowing you to ponder. As we all know, nothing in this life is permanent. If problems exist at one time, they will vanish at a later time.

- **Take a walk.**

Walking makes you cheerful all of the time. It helps to prevent cardiac problems and is also beneficial for weight loss. So, anytime you have free time, take a walk. Make it a habit to go for a morning walk.

- **Maintain hydration.**

Water aids in the regulation of metabolism and the reduction of ageing signs. People always recommend that you drink water before each meal and then wait an hour before drinking another glass of water after meal. Always drink a warm glass of water when you first wake up in the morning to help your metabolism.

- **Instill good habits in your children.**

Taking a bath early thing in the morning will keep you and your child fresh throughout the day.

It is beneficial for students because their focus improves. In the mornings, many of the students have been spotted lazing in the apartment without bathing. They take a bath at 11 or 12 p.m. in the afternoon. It's a bad habit to get into.

C. Instill the habit of taking a bath first thing in the morning in your children.

C. Teach them to offer water to the Sun God and Gayatri mantra, a potent chant for increasing cerebral capacity in children.
C. Teach them to touch the feet of the elders. These positive habits, if ingrained in a child, will help him grow into a successful adult.

- **Incorporate yoga into your daily routine.**

Yoga Pranayams assist you manage your weight, blood pressure, thyroid, PCOD, and other issues.

Many people have reduced weight and regulated thyroid, blood pressure, and other conditions by practicing Pranayams such Kapalabhati, Anulom Vilom, and Bhastrika.

Some asanas, such as **Bhujang asana** and **Ushtra asana**, can help women with cyclic problems regulate their menstrual cycle.

- **Do not sit for long hours**

If you have an office work or you are working in a shop where you have to sit or stand for long hours. Then, practice stretching exercises at regular intervals or take a stroll around your office room or store to keep your blood circulating and maintain your health.

Remember, your health is in your hands. If you practice these good habits, you find that life is more than beautiful when your health is okay. Your relationships are going to improve once you are mentally and physically strong, trust me.

Some Exercises for you

- Sleep early to get up early.
- Make a target to sleep 7 hours.
- Practice Yoga in the morning.
- If possible, take a 20 or 30 minutes walk daily. If not outside. Do it in room.
- Drink water 15 minutes before having food and one hour after your food.
- Keep your mobile phones away when you are free and spend time with your family or follow your passion .

Summary

1. Take up good habits to keep yourself focused.
2. Keep yourself hydrated.
3. Go for a walk.
4. Teach your children good habits.

CHAPTER FIVE

COUNT YOUR BLESSINGS

Let us start with a story.

Once there was a millionaire who used to travel in a very expensive car of his own. One day on social media, he saw that one of his top stars of whom he was a fan, had purchased a helicopter. He started desiring a helicopter and told his manager that he too wanted to have one and that he was fed up of traveling in a car. The manager immediately told him "But sir, you have got the most expensive car in the entire city." Still, that man did not seem satisfied with what he had.

Suddenly, someone knocked at his car window and asked," Is this Rolls Royce car? I longed to have this car it is such a beautiful and luxurious car". These words immediately changed the mindset of that millionaire and he started feeling grateful for his luxurious car.

The man who had knocked at the car window, came back to his car which was an Ambassador car, of which he was fed up. He just kicked at the car and said that he was fed up of driving in that car. He wished to have more money to buy the Rolls Royce car. As he was kicking his car, a lady came by and asked him what the matter was, was his car broken down to which he answered that he was fed up with his car and that he wanted to buy a luxurious car.

At this point, the lady told him that he should be thankful that at least he had a car to commute from one place to another faster. While she had to take a bus to commute to her office. That man immediately realized that at least he had an ambassador car and he should be thankful for it. While that lady was standing at the bus stand, she missed the bus. She was frustrated.

When a person came by on his cycle and asked her why was she upset. She told him that she had missed the bus and every time she has to come to the bus stand for taking a bus to commute to her office. That boy said that at least she did not have to ride a bicycle; she has got a bus to move faster, to her destination, while he travels around 10 miles from his house to office and then back to his house on a bicycle. At this, she realized that she has at least the facility of a bus to move around.

When this person on bicycle moved forward, he kicked his bicycle and stated that he was tired of moving the paddles with his feet on that bicycle. When he came across a woman sitting in a wheelchair, she inquired as to what his problem was. Was his bicycle broken down? To which he told her that he no longer enjoyed riding his bicycle. He was tired of riding his bicycle and wished for a two-wheeler, to which the lady replied that he should be grateful that he had a bicycle with which he could commute. She did not have any legs as she had met with an accident and had lost her legs.

Immediately this person with bicycle started realizing that whatever he had was quite enough. It was more than enough, which he did not ever ask in his life.

What do you learn from this story? Don't you have things around you that you couldn't ever ask and it is still available with you? Look around yourself and see what things are available, with you for which you should be grateful.

• If you own a home, you should be thankful that you don't have to pay rent for it.

- If you're stuck at a job, at the very least you should be thankful that you have a job.

- If you are a businessman, even if it doesn't always run smoothly, at least you have recognition in society.

• If your children are obedient, even though they might not be doing well in school. They are, nevertheless, submissive to you. They also do not hang around like other boys.

Isn't it true that you should be grateful and content with what you have?

- If you have a loving husband, though he may not be earning much, he loves you so much and cares for you. Isn't that more than enough for a lady to have and be contented with?

Instead of comparing your life with your neighbors or with other people, look at yourself, look at your life, what things you have for which you should be grateful to nature and to the Almighty.

Maybe the things that you do not have or you lack, you do not deserve them, or maybe those things do not deserve you. Whatever you are getting is with the grace of the Almighty.

God knows better than you what to give you and what not to give you.

Remember life is a difficult exam. Here everybody has a different question paper. You cannot copy or imitate the answers of the other person into your own question paper.

Everybody has a different life. Some people may have a car and you may be longing for it. But maybe they might have taken a car on monthly EMI and have to pay for it for several months.

A rich person may have a palatial house, but maybe it is on a mortgage to pay his debts, maybe he is running in losses. You never know what the other person is going through.

So instead of looking at people who are at a higher position than you, just look at the people who are below you, who are poor but still contented in their life.

Haven't you ever seen the people living in slums, how their children are happy having a satisfactory smile on their faces? This is because they are contented with their life. They know how to enjoy their lives. They know what they have and they are always grateful for it.

It may be that they are having some scarcity of food or clothes, but still, they are united. They do not compare themselves with others. So instead of looking at people, higher than you, it's better to look at your blessings, the countless blessings that nature has provided you.

If you have a family who loves you and stands by you in all difficult situations, this is more than anything else as a blessing for you. This is the best gift that God has given you which may be several people are longing for and suffering in the families.

If at times your business is running in losses, or it may not be running well. Don't be discouraged at least your family is there to cooperate with you. If you have saved some money for the urgent times, you can be thankful to God that you have at least something to eat and to wear .

There are many people who still do not have shelter. They have nothing to eat and they die just like that on the streets in the severely cold winters or in the stroking heat of summers.

At times, you may be missing your trip or a flight and you may get frustrated. But always think that whatever happens is with the will of God.

Allow me to tell you another different story.

Once there was a Heart specialist. He was required to fly to Mumbai for a Medical Conference. As a result, he had to board a plane, but the flight had to be postponed due to terrible weather. It was also rescheduled until the next day. But he had to make it to the conference on the same day at all costs.

Someone advised him that he could take a taxi to get to his location swiftly. As a result, he took a taxi, and the weather began to deteriorate in the meantime. Since the driver couldn't see any further, the cab had to come to a rest somewhere in the middle. When the doctor turned to look around, he observed a little cottage.

He knocked on the door and entered . There was an elderly woman praying to God, as well as a young kid who was resting on a cot and appeared to be extremely unwell. She greeted him and handed him a glass of water. The doctor requested her to provide him with refuge until the weather improved.

She offered him whatever food she had prepared at home, as well as some Prasad that she had offered to God. The doctor inquired about her grandson's whereabouts. "I was praying to God about my grandchild," she explained. "He has a problem with his heart. Dr. Massoud, a cardiac expert, according to some sources, can treat my child, nobody else. So I am praying to God to make some situations so that I can meet Dr. Massoud".

Suddenly, the doctor started crying because he himself was, Dr. Massoud. He told her that her prayers have been answered to by God. "Owing to bad weather conditions, God has shown me the direction to your house. So you don't have to worry and I will treat your child", said the Doctor.

What does this is story show? This story shows that whatever God wills only those things occur in our life. He also knows what the right time to fulfill what we desire.

If you try to attain higher positions by wrong means, they are not everlasting. And we all know that nothing is permanent in this life. Whatever things we are earning, whatever money we are earning, whatever relations we are earning, whatever name we are earning, we all have to leave them here. One day we will go empty-handed only with our deeds.

So always be satisfied with what you have and be thankful to God for whatever he has given you. I am not saying that you should not work hard to attain high position, but never take a wrong path to achieve your goals. Always try to be an upright person in your life. Though you may not be having enough, at least you have that much which other people desire. So always Count your blessings and feel blessed every moment of your life.

Small Exercise for You

- Every morning when you wake up, thank God for waking you healthy and opportunity to live another day.
- Always try to be honest and hardworking to achieve your goals. Do not take wrong Path.
- Look at people who are lower than you in position and be grateful for what you have.
- If you have good children, and are doing okay at school, be thankful for that as they are at least learning something in Life.
- If you are troubled, turn your attention to good aspects of your life and gradually you will find solution to your problem.

Summary

1. Always be thankful for whatever you have and smile for those things which you had never asked for.
2. If things do not happen according to you, then it is because God knows better what to give you and what not .
3. Work hard and honestly to achieve your goals.
4. Whatever we are earning on this earth, will be left here except for our deeds.
5. Everybody's life is different from one another, so do not compare your life with the life of others.

Remember life is a difficult exam. Here everybody has a different question paper. You cannot copy or imitate the answers of the other person into your own question paper.

CHAPTER SIX

SPEND TIME WITH YOURSELF

In this busy life and all the hustle and bustle around us, we are bound to fulfill all our obligations. That too 24/7 just fulfilling the dreams of our family members or working hard to please our bosses.

In all this, we nearly forget ourselves. We nearly forget we are also humans, and we need some time for ourselves. Take a break. Think about the rat race you are in. Where is it leading you? Are you aware of yourself? Are you aware what do you want? What does your body need?

You will have no answer as you have never ever thought about yourself in this way. You did not feel any urge to take care of yourself or spend time with yourself.

But I must tell you being always surrounded by family members does not help you in understanding yourself. So take out some time for yourself. Switch off your phones. Stay away from all, just you and only you should be there.

1. By staying with yourself you can analyze your weaknesses and strengths and work on your weakness.

1. You feel more calm and relaxed as it would be like you were waiting for this time to relax mentally, physically and emotionally.

3. You can even just sit idle doing nothing. No phones, no cinemas, no talking, no watching television just sitting idle, which will relieve your stress. This will make you understand your inner self.

4. You feel more energetic and refreshed and you feel like now you can give hundred percent to your family and handle the problems easily.

5. You can sit beside your window, having a cup of coffee or tea and enjoying the atmosphere. What an excellent date!

6. This is the time when you can realize your past mistakes and even try to rectify them or make a promise not to do it again. You get a better understanding of your character.

7. Spend time in doing creative things that you could not ever find time to do. Like carrying out your passion of writing poems, singing, painting, dancing, get time to think and analyze your progress and failures in life. Read your favorite book which you have ever longed to read.

8. You become happier and focused more to your own thoughts and feelings. This is a part of self-care.

9. Take out time for you to hang out at a restaurant, park or cinema. It may sound selfish but, yes, I am sure you will enjoy your own company. And this elixir of your life should be drunk only by you.

10. Try to discover the real you. What are your desires? Who are you? You would get to explore yourself closely.

So take out time once or twice a month and spend time with yourself. You will enjoy this moment of life with yourself.

Remember; don't be lost in the crowd of life. Try to find yourself, the real you. For those who are in a habit of remaining in a group and do not like spending time alone. They can take only initial five minutes in order to stay with themselves. And then gradually the time can be increased.

"Sometimes sitting silently and enjoying one's company is the most wonderful feeling that anyone can have in this world"

Pritma

Some Exercises for You

- Take out time for yourself once a month or a week.
- Keep away your smart phones and enjoy the beauty of nature.

- Try to make a diary and write all your weaknesses on which you have to work upon.
- Try to know your inner self by taking up meditations.

Summary

1. Sometimes we have to take out time for ourselves ,instead of running in the rat race.
2. Enjoy your time with yourself reading, writing, painting etc.
3. Try to know your real self and desires .Explore your real self.SPE

CHAPTER SEVEN

ACCEPT YOUR FAILURES EQUALLY AS YOUR SUCCESS

Assume you are starting a business and want to earn a profit on your investment. After a few days, you realize that everything has been a complete disaster. The result of the input you gave was not received.

What would your reaction be if you were in this situation?

You would be downcast, sad, and unsatisfied with your life. You would believe it had completely ruined your life and squandered all of your effort, time, and excitement.

You wish you could go back and undo everything. This is life, my dear, and there are no undos, or delete buttons to get things back to the way they were.

Some words would echo in your ears and mind ,"Failure! You are a loser. Your life is a waste “. These thoughts continuously keep pricking you from within. You feel as if you are in deep waters from where there is no way to come out.

“You always pass failure on your way to success”

Mickey Rooney

Here, I must tell you that failures are the first step to success .Failure is not the end ,but the beginning of your journey to success.

“Successful people don’t fear failure but understand that it’s necessary to learn and grow from”

Robert Kiyosaki

You should accept your failures as your teachers that help you know your mistakes. You will gradually learn never to commit such mistakes, but will try to rectify your way of taking decisions. Trust me, you will never have to look back. Though it will be a journey of hurdles, but you will enjoy all the difficulties if you take your failures positively.

The amazing example that we can observe from Indian history is how our leaders were dedicated to achieving independence from the British.

Many revolts erupted against the British, but no one gave up since they had learned from their previous failures and were ready to fight the British once more. Many leaders gave their lives and many innocent people died in the process, but they all had the same goal: to achieve independence and declare India a free country.

Their persistent efforts have resulted in us breathing the fresh air of 73 years of independence.

So, if they could make it, why do we get dejected over a single setback in life? Why don't we return with more vigor and enthusiasm?

"Success and Failures are part of our journey. Enjoy your failures equally as you enjoy your success. Learn from your failures and achieve success in life:"

Pritma

Let's see an inspiring story of the founder of **KFC. Colonel Sanders.**

When he was six years old, his father passed away, and Sanders had to cook and care for his siblings. When he was in seventh class, he had to drop out of the school in order to take work as a farmhand.

At 16, he got a job in United States Army by altering his age on papers. He lost the job in a year's span. Then he got a job in the railways as a laborer. While working on the railways, he studied law, but it ruined his entire career of legal practice when he got into another fight.

So he had to move back with his mom and he got a job as a life insurance agent. There also he got fired for insubordination which means he could not submit to whatever they said. But he was a guy with a firm determination.

In 1920, he started earning well, when he started a ferry company. Then he started a business to create a lamp. This business utterly faced failure as he learned that another company had a better version of this lamp.

At 40, he started selling chicken dishes at a service station. And when he advertised his food again, he entered into an argument with a competitor, which was a deadly shootout.

Four years later, he came back with a bang, and bought a motel. This motel burned to the ground along with his restaurant, but this guy wouldn't give up.

Instead of taking his failures negatively, he took them positively, and he ran a new motel until World War Two forced him to close it down.

After the war, he attempted to franchise his restaurant, but the public turned down his dish. They turned down his recipe 1009 times, but he persisted. Sanders coined the phrase "Kentucky Fried Chicken" to describe his secret recipe. It is currently known as KFC. However, due to the construction of an interstate near the eatery, it was forced to close. So Sanders had to sell that business, but he kept his promise to expand KFC franchisees and hire KFC employees across the country.

He had to suffer lots of failures and misfortunes all throughout his life. When finally he hit a big and expanded internationally and sold the company for $2 billion. Even today, we see they put the picture of Sanders in the logo of KFC branding. He passed away at 90 because of pneumonia. By that time, there were 60000 KFC locations in 48 countries.

So what do you guys get by it? You feel dejected, depressed, discouraged at small failures in your life. But this guy who had constantly faced failures in his life, never gave up.

Isn't it inspiring, that this man who at his old age could gain success did not give up and was working continuously throughout his life?

So remember, your failures are the stepping stones to gain success.

Since we are humans, not God, so it's okay if we fail, we will get up and start our journey again.

Some Exercise for You

- Do not be afraid to take risks. Even if you fail, you will learn something.
- If you do not get success in your ventures, do not consider it as an end. Think about it with cool mind and try for it again.
- Do not mind people who will mock at your failures. Instead Pat your back ,that you have the courage to face your failures.

Summary

1. You should accept your failures as your teachers that help you know your mistakes.

2. Even if you fail in your efforts, do not be dejected, rise up with vigor and try again.

3. Failures are the stepping stones to gain success as they make you an experienced person.

4. It is okay if we fail, we will get up and start our journey again.

CHAPTER EIGHT

ACCEPT YOUR OLD AGE WHOLEHEARTEDLY

Old Age is not a bane, but a boon. Many people are afraid of old age, as they cannot accept the transformation because they're apprehensive of the future and of their appearance. But you should accept it wholeheartedly.

"Old age is not the end, but a start of your new journey to cherish your unfulfilled dreams of your of youth. "

Pritma

Believe me, this is a phase of life where you can relax and cherish your desires that you could not fulfill in your youth because of responsibilities. Many people become aware of the looks or appearance and try applying creams, take medicines, or injections to keep them young. Please do not do this. Be natural as you are. If you are young at heart, age does not matter. Your emotions will naturally reflect on your face, making it glow and look younger than anyone else of your age.

Remember, accepting what you are will really move you on to a new journey. You do not have to depend on others for compliments. Look at yourself in the mirror and feel yourself beautiful and it will reflect on your appearance. Your thoughts reflect what you are.

It is claimed that old age is like youth since you can now fulfill all of your aspirations that you couldn't when you were younger.

1. Make time to see your friends, share memories, and have little parties and celebrations with them.

You will appreciate this phase of life because you are in the same age group.

2. Do something creative whatever you wish to do which you could not do when you were in your youth. You have time now, like painting, reading, poetry writing. It will make you mentally sharp.

3. **It is okay if you cannot wear tight clothes,** you can wear clothes that make you feel comfortable. Do not mind what other people say about your appearance.

4. **If you are having any disease** or pain in muscles or bones, you can give time to yourself and do certain exercises to reduce the intensity of the pain. Consult a doctor to know what steps to take.

5. It is imperative that you keep your limbs moving. So always take a walk in the morning, after lunch or after dinner, to keep you active.

6. **Implement yoga in your daily routine**. Pranayams like Kapalabhati,Anulom Vilom and Bhastrika can help you cure diseases like diabetes, thyroid blood pressure, and they can also regulate your weight.

7. **Go to a park** and enjoy the scene over there. See the nature the innocent faces of children and pay gratitude to nature to give you an opportunity to be in a beautiful company.

8. **Avoid situations** that create stress and tensions as they may be harmful to your health.

9. **Listen to music**. Music therapy is the best therapy to bring a smile on your face. If you're suffering with a disease, listening to music can help you focus your attention from your pain and suffering to the essence of that music which will help you cure faster.

10. **Do meditation.** Doing a 10 minute meditation morning and night will relieve your stress and make you calm. You get to know yourself in a better way.

11. **Do laughter therapy. This** therapy will increase the flow of blood and also boost up your self-confidence.

12. **Remain in the company of people who make you feel happy**.

13. **Maintain your self-esteem in the family** and do not interfere in the lives of your sons or daughters who are married. Be available to them when they need your advice. But be sure not to impose your ideas or advice on them forcefully. Let them take their own decisions and you will automatically be relieved of all tensions regarding the future.

You can also be with them to celebrate the success or be with them to support them when they are passing through difficult phase of life.

14. **Remember, old age is not always welcomed** by all the members of the family. You might be a burden on them. So do not transfer your property so early to any of them. It might sound rude, but yes, the money you have saved will be the only support of your old age to help you live a decent life even if your family members ditch you.

15. **You can use your skills and experience** to teach people around you to help them become self dependent. If you see a smile on their faces due to your effort, you feel that this is the best way of living a life.

You can appreciate the beauty of life and treasure your unfulfilled desires while also taking care to free yourself of all stress and worries. Because now is the time for your children to have the life that you did, and you must be free of all your worries about them. Allow them to make their own decisions and control their own fate. You won't be able to be with them all of the time. So let them go, and you'll be pleased because you'll be able to fulfill all of your unfulfilled wishes.

Summary

1. Enjoy your old age and fulfill your desires of youth.
2. Do something creative.
3. Share your skills and Experience with people by teaching them
4. Maintain your self-esteem in the family and let your children make decisions.
5. Enjoy with people of your age group
6. Do Yoga and Exercises to keep you healthy
7. Do laughter therapy to keep you smiling.

CHAPTER NINE

LET GO OFF PEOPLE WHO DON'T CARE

Samaira was upset as she was constantly checking her WhatsApp but did not receive a single message from Thomas, her love, since morning. She kept wondering, "What is the reason? Why he did not answer to my good morning message?"

Thomas usually used to revert to her good morning message every day. She had sent him good morning wishes at 6:30 AM. As soon as she woke up, she noticed Thomas had read her message but did not reply.

The Adverse behavior of Thomas took aback her.

She messaged him, asking the reason for not talking to her, but to no avail. In the afternoon, she messaged him, "despite all your awkward behavior, I still love you from the deepest core of my heart". Still, she did not receive any response. This was not the first time Thomas had done this to Samira. Every time she had to apologize, not knowing the reason.

This time she decided she would not communicate with him anymore. Thomas was not the right person to spend her life with. Do you know what she did? She closed her eyes and said, "I forgive you. May God bless you. May you be healthy".

Guys, did you see she acknowledged her love and emotions for Thomas and did not replace her feelings with hatred? Instead, she took the path of walking away and forgiving him.

Remember, it is better to walk away from the person who does not care for your feelings or even does not answer your questions. Our relationship should be as transparent as water and if you feel your partner is not being transparent, it is better to end up the relationship and practice self-love.

Improve your self-esteem, because, in this world, nobody cares for you except you.

"If you love and respect yourself, you are already a worthy person you do not need others to tell you your actual worth"

Pritma

Do not look at others to give you a report card that you are worthy or you need some improvement. No human is perfect. We all have some flaws in us. We have to learn to accept those flaws and work on them.

Complete dependability on the partner is the biggest flaw in a relationship. Soon they feel they cannot live without a partner and have no existence without one.

Let me tell you, if you are honest to yourself, then you do not need anybody in this world to complete you. We are all complete in ourselves. We do not need any partners. Since childhood, our parents have always taught us that when we grow up, we have to get married and we need a life partner to support us throughout our life.

Have you ever seen the "Ardhnarishwar" form of Lord Shiva, where Shiva and Parvati are right and left body parts of Lord Shiva?

Every human has within himself both man and woman. It shows that we are complete in ourselves. We have seen many women more strict than male police officers like Kiran Bedi, who has proved her power.

If you face treachery with your partner, leave them and practice the art of loving yourself and spending time with those who love you and care for you.

Keep yourself busy with some work. Do not avoid your emotions, as it may create toxicity in you.

If you feel angry, express it. If you feel like crying, cry to your heart and then move on and show your strength in some field where you can keep your mind busy.

Go out, spend some time with yourself and give yourself time. Take opportunities to visit new people. Take up new adventurous tasks or challenging tasks to keep yourself engaged and excited. Gradually, with time, you notice that the person now does not matter in your life. Maybe, some other person is waiting for you who will love you truly and care for you.

After all, life is an ever-flowing river, where the past is left behind, and you progress further. So take life positively and make it beautiful. It is in your hands to shift your focus from your problems to something adventurous, and your problems will gradually fade away.

Summary

1. Leave people who do not care for you and focus your attention to those who love you.
2. Do not control your emotions as it can lead to toxicity.
3. Take up challenges to keep yourself busy.
1.

CHAPTER TEN

STAY AWAY FROM TOO MUCH AVARICE

We as humans are greedy from birth. As a child, we are greedy to receive attention of our parents. So we either cry or we do something nice to get their attention and love. At school, we are greedy about receiving appreciation of our teachers. And so we study hard. When we pass out school to get to our desired goal we have agreed from our parents to spend for higher education. When we graduate, we have greed or desire to get a good job.

When we are in a job, we are in desire to get a promotion and for this we do everything to get a promotion. It is normal to be greedy, to achieve our goals is not bad. But when we become blind by the urge to earn more and more money, we actually forget that this is not the proper way of living.

The basic needs of a human are food, clothing and shelter and if you have all this, despite which you are running after money and neglecting your family. Can you imagine where you are heading to? Most of you would say education has become costly. So we have to earn to educate our children. Things have become costly, so we have to earn to meet the expenses. Okay, agreed

Is it necessary to spend money on unnecessary things? Just to show off people that your status is high or just to make someone jealous. Years later, you realize that you had spent half of your life to get the things which are not even necessary. And in that pursuit, you have lost some valuable relations. You have lost some valuable moments of your life which you could have spent with your family and your children.

Sometimes people are so jealous that they would suggest that you invest money in schemes that would fetch lucrative profit to you. In that greed, sometimes we are so much caught that we invest a good amount of our hard earned money in it and ultimately face failures.

Sometimes, you may find some luring offers with links sent on your WhatsApp messages. If you click on those links after being moved by it, the money you had is already in the hands of the cheaters. This is cybercrime.

Some time back, I had done online shopping on **Snap deal**. A few days later, a phone call came telling me that since I had done shopping on the app, I have won the first prize for the Tata Indica car, I immediately refused it as these phone calls ask us to fill out a form with all our personal details and also deposit some amount of money to get a prize.

What I suggest is simple living, and high thinking should be the formula of every human being. Because what we have on this earth, we ultimately have to leave everything. So try finding peace of mind. Amidst the rat race of earning money,.

"Money can buy everything but not peace of mind."

The true nature of man is to live a peaceful life. You can do things like

1. On weekends, if possible, spend time with yourself and your family. Keep away your smart phones.
2. Spend money on only those things which are necessary
3. Dispose of unnecessary things and create a space in your room and mind.

4. Try helping people around you and you will get satisfaction. The more you help others, the more peace you find in your soul.

5. Save the hard earned money for emergency purposes.

6. Teach your children how to work hard and save money. Do not satisfy all the demands, even if you're rich. Teach them the importance of money.

1. Show gratitude for all you have.

Summary

1. Greed is okay to achieve goals to some extent.
2. Do not spend too much money to show off to people.
3. Spend money only on things that are necessary.
4. Do not run after greed to such an extent that you might miss some valuable moments of your life.

5. Dispose of unwanted things and create space in your room and mind.

CHAPTER ELEVEN

STOP EXPECTING FROM ANYONE

Expectations are the root cause of all miseries. The more we expect from others, the more we depend on them for all our achievements. This reduces our self confidence. The belief that we have in our self is shaken up. For example if we expect others to praise us for how we look then we should be prepared for appreciation and criticism as well. You cannot always expect others to appreciate you as you want them to. Every person has his own point of view and the way of looking at things. They always cannot get into your shoes and do as you want them to .

- Do not expect people to understand you- if you cannot explain yourself clearly then people will never understand you. You cannot expect them to support you without understanding your point of view or your feelings. Nobody knows each other's real situation. So be clear and specific.
- **Stop expecting people to be your support** always. If you are wrong then definitely even your loved ones will not support your decisions or actions. They will give you suggestions to rectify your mistakes which you have to accept positively.
- **Stop expecting your partner to give you time** if you want to be happy stop expecting love and time from your partner if he or she is busy and has no time for you try to maintain your dignity by showing self importance and keep yourself busy with some hobbies exercises reading at 17 do not run for his attention.
- **Stop expecting your first job or business to be the best** If you have started with a business or job always be prepared for failures also give

your hundred percent and do not expect anything

- In times of needs also, do not expect anyone to help you or ask you about your well being. You have to be your own support.
- **Stop expecting everyday to be the best**. There can be days when things can go wrong but it does not mean that everything is over. Enjoy the problems and try to take out some solutions for it.

Remember, every man is capable enough to be his own support and be independent. Depending on others and expecting them to do whatever you want, is your weakness and when things do not turn up as you wanted them then you are plunged in sorrow.

Summary

ax. Do not expect people to understand you without your point being made clear to them.
ax. Do not expect everyday to be the same.
ax. Do not expect people to help you in times of need.

Do not expect your loved ones to take your side even if you are wrong

Concluding Remarks

We all go through various stages of life and have to face various types of hurdles like relationship problems, getting into bad habits very easily.

In the need of earning money, sometimes we forget to spend valuable time with our family .Sometimes we forget that we too are humans and need time for ourselves also.

In addition to this, we also expect others to help us and if they do not do so, we are plunged in sorrow. These expectations are generally the root causes of our miseries. I took all these concepts to be compiled in the form of a book.

Although there are various ways to be happy. I have covered only 11 points to help at least some people who are facing such problems.

Your comments are welcome. jashpritma@gmail.com

About The Author

Pritma Jashnani, is the head of **Centre of Computer Technology**,Lucknow, who has taught several students so far in her career of 25 years.

She has taught more than 3000 students who are now successfully placed in top companies.She has a unique style of teaching. She believes in quality education rather than increasing quantity of students.

She has been teaching courses like

Java, Website Designing, Data Structures, Python,Android and a lot more to Btech,MCA and BCA students.

13 years back, she started writing books for her students so that they do not find any difficulty in the topics they are taught.

She took a lot of time doing research and picking questions from the exam papers of various schools and compiling them into set of two both for class 10th and 12th.

Study Material and Exercise book.

She has also written books on **ASP.NET , PHP, PYTHON,Core Java, C#, Advanced Java,Oracle etc.**

This is her first book on non-fiction series which she had been thinking about from the last so many years.

Under the guidance of the two Famous Authors **Inspiring Jatin** and **Sweta Samota**, she received a pushback to write all her thoughts in the form of this book which she is presenting to you.

She is now writing another book, which will be released soon.

Hope you like this book as it will encourage her to write more books for you.

A. For Joining any courses ,you can contact her by sending mail on jashpritma@gmail.com

C. You can even buy any study materials on **Java,ANDROID,ASP.NET,C,C++,C#,PHP etc.**

About The Centre Centre Of Computer Technology

Offers courses like

1. CERTIFICATE IN OFFICE AUTOMATION
2. DIPLOMA IN COMPUTER STUDIES
3. DIPLOMA IN JAVA PROGRAMMING
4. DIPLOMA IN DOT NET TECHNNOLOGY
5. FULL STACK WEB DEVELOPMENT

VARIOUS SHORT TERM COURSES ALSO
YOU CAN CONTACT ON
jashpritma@gmail.com

Printed by Libri Plureos GmbH in Hamburg,
Germany